WORDS

as Definitions
of Experience

Arnold Wesker

with an afterword by
Richard Appignanesi

Writers and Readers Publishing Cooperative

Words as Definitions of Experience

First published in Great Britain by
The Writers and Readers Publishing Cooperative,
14 Talacre Road, London NW5 3PE
in 1976

ISBN 0 904613 26 7

Arnold Wesker's writings include the plays, *The Kitchen, Chicken Soup With Barley, Roots, I'm Talking About Jerusalem, Chips With Everything, The Four Seasons, Their Very Own and Golden City, The Friends, The Old Ones, The Journalists, The Wedding Feast,* and most recently *The Merchant,* scheduled to open in New York and London in 1977. Wesker's other writings include *Fears of Fragmentation* (essays); *Six Sundays in January* (short stories, plays, etc.); *Love Letters on Blue Paper* (short stories); *Say Goodbye: You May Never See Them Again* (text with paintings by John Allin). For television, Wesker has written *Menace* and most recently, *Love Letters on Blue Paper.*

All performing rights of Arnold Wesker's plays are fully protected, and permission to perform, whether by amateurs or professionals, must be obtained in advance from Robin Dalton, 18 Elm Tree Road, London NW8, who can furnish all particulars.

Richard Appignanesi is a writer and a founder-member of the Writers and Readers Publishing Cooperative.

WORDS
as Definitions
of Experience

Arnold Wesker

"Not to be a poet is the worst of all our miseries"

Introduction

I will begin with a story.

One day my eldest son, aged thirteen then, was standing outside his school talking to some friends. It's a local school with a 70% immigrant and working-class population. He's a big boy, who — it was three years ago — had very long hair and those irritatingly happy, intelligent eyes. Two older boys from the school approached him. One kicked him in the back-side. He ignored the kick. 'Get stuffed!' said the other boy to him. 'Alright, I will,' replied my obliging son, and he continued to ignore the two fourth-formers. 'Get stuffed!' said the other boy again. My son assured him, confidently, that as he'd promised, he *would* 'get stuffed'. The boy drew back his arm and with a heavy ringed fist smashed into my son's right eye. 'Good God!' said my son, reeling back, unable to believe anyone could do that or that it could happen to him. And then he came home.

His bewilderment is perhaps what distressed me most. It seemed to him to have no logic, no reason, no point. He couldn't account for it.

He was not equipped with those concepts of human behaviour which might have enabled him to place their actions within a pattern of behaviour recognisable enough for him to have worked out some effective or self-reassuring response. Words contain within them concepts of human behaviour. He was not equipped with such words.

Therefore, because it's understood that words transmit concepts of human experience, the concern in this brief article is twofold: to offer an argument in defence of words — the importance of which is being ignored and their value eroded— and to offer a suggestion to the education establishment of the country. The article will attempt to reaffirm the value of the use of language by the artist, and argue for the imperative need of teachers to use, explain and equip their pupils with words in a way that will enable them to use language effectively. By effectively I mean very specifically: language as a conceptual means of identifying and defining experience.

Let me be even more specific and say what I mean by 'experience'. My concern is to defend language as a means of both naming and comprehending the implications of the experience of *what is being done to one, and what one is doing to others.* And I believe it is the teacher who must help identify and define experience by using language in a special subject set aside in the school curriculum, and that he must do so with the aid of the works of artists. All this I hope will become clear as this simple, rudimentary pamphlet develops.

Words

For those of us living in the West, these are difficult times in which not to be confused and intimidated. Guilts are there to be felt daily, and many are there to ensure we feel guilty. So much so that I sometimes wonder whether ensuring the guilt of others in some way assuages one's own! With so much of the world underprivileged, dare anyone still claim a priority for the place of the teacher and the artist? Yes, for the teacher who trains mechanics and doctors, and the artist who can illustrate slogans. But for the teacher who trains sensibilities, sharpens our critical judgements? For the artist who deepens our perceptions? The practical use of such study is rarely understood, more often it's actively scorned.

It is a curious fact that large sections of the bourgeoisie and certain elements in the militant Left share with the Nazis this strange loathing which moves them to reach for their guns at the mention of culture. (I use the word 'culture' in this context because it's commonly recognised; personally I prefer the distinction that is made between art and culture — the latter being used to describe the entire life-style of a society of which art is only one part. The Nazis, of course, were using culture to mean that they hated all but a narrow field of propaganda art and pseudo-scholarship.)

The following disturbing anecdote illustrates this contempt for genuine art and scholarship. The British playwrights David Mercer and John Arden, both known for their (albeit idiosyncratic) Marxist positions, were once invited to lecture in

Sussex University — a university known for its student militancy. They were barely given a hearing. Stink bombs together with abuse were hurled at them. Later, a student approached Mercer and said, 'We must burn all the books, start again, from the beginning, burn them all.'

'What?' asked Mercer, gently, 'Marx and Engels as well?'

'All of them!' cried the student. 'Burn them all!'

'Excuse me,' said Mercer, 'but that worries me a little, for the last time people said that was in the days of the Reichstag.'

'The *what?*' asked the student.

About two years ago an Arab friend visited me. She had once been involved in the theatre but now, between professional commitments, was deeply engaged in Arab politics, a reassessment of which had been brought about by the ill-conceived and senseless Arab-Israeli war. 'I now believe all art to be irrelevant,' she said. It was a familiar refrain. I had some sympathy with the feeling but felt angrily opposed to where it led her.

Every time art and scholarship are thrown out of the window it is because people have found their emotional, ethical, or intellectual demands too bothersome to contend with. The gun becomes a simpler solution. And because it is a simpler solution it is enthusiastically taken up by the simple-minded, and the times become frightening. It is easier and — to begin with — more glamorous to be a heroic man of action than a thoughtful man of letters. The act of pulling a trigger takes less time than thinking a thought through. Its effect is immediate; it commands the attention of greater numbers — or their fearful obedience, at least — and it appears to reflect greater courage. Where four-fifths of the world are under-nourished, they are also under-educated, and there the report of a gun is a language more comprehensible and accessible than, say, the words of the poet Shelley who reported that he:

'. . . met a traveller from an antique land
Who said: Two vast and trunkless legs of stone
Stand in the desert . . .'

Shelley is telling us about a great King upon whose statue were inscribed these words:

' "My name is Ozymandias, King of Kings;
Look upon my words ye mighty, and despair."
Nothing beside remains. Round the decay
Of that colossal wreck, boundless and bare
The lone and level sands stretch far away.'

Personally I consider the long-term potential of such a
poem, which suggests historical perspective, withers the fear of
tyrants and minimises the possibility of their emergence, to be
more effective than a bullet. But nevertheless, most of us
understand or feel intimidated when huge numbers respond to
such a simple tongue as a gun. *I* certainly sympathize. And yet
I despise it.

I do not believe in the simple wisdom of the people. That
has always seemed to me insulting and patronizing, stirring the
heart of the one who utters it but commanding little more than
ephemeral loyalties from those it briefly flatters. I do, however,
believe in the ability of the deprived and wretched to confront
and assimilate knowledge and art — and *through* them to become
wise. (I say 'through them' by way of suggesting that though
experience is often the first and most powerful teacher, yet it is
not sacrosanct. Experience frequently distorts judgements and
needs help to be illuminated.)

The courage and intelligence of George Jackson, one of the
Soledad brothers, form a saga I shall remember for a long time,
reminding me of the cancerous evil the United States has still
to cut out from itself; but even intelligent men have loose
tongues that produce a rhetoric which lesser men become
intoxicated with and misuse. Jackson's cry 'Let the voice of our
guns express the words of our freedom' must be such a
comfortable slogan for lazy minds to live with. Similarly, Che
Guevara was an honourable man, a real hero, a man to be loved
and yet, paradoxically, he unleashed much mindlessness into
the world with his cry to 'hate! hate! hate!' I can't bring myself
to be grateful for that.

To my Arab friend I sent a copy of a poem by the late
Francis Hope (killed in the terrible Paris air crash on March 2nd,
1974).
In it are some lines I'd like to have written:

'At times like these, he cried aloud
That not to be a poet is
The worst of all our miseries . . .'

'*Not* to be a poet is the worst of all our miseries . . .' I think
I'll always feel that. (And of course I'm using the name 'poet' in
its widest sense — all artists have a touch of the poet in them.
The greatest have more poet than journalist, the lesser have more
journalist than poet. But that's another debate entirely, fraught
with another set of dangers!)

I know of course that in times of great evil not to be a poet
and not to have a gun is a double misery. But — and here we may
begin to see, at last, why understanding of the word is so
essential — evil must be carefully measured and accurately named.
We must be absolutely certain the times are evil and not
something else or we might find ourselves drawing blood to
drown a fly, when to spit would be enough.

For example: were Hitler and Nixon both evil men?
Wouldn't it be more precise to say Hitler was evil, Nixon was
corrupt? Isn't it necessary to distinguish between the evil of a
Stalin and the authoritarianism, perhaps cynicism, of a Brezhnev?
Or let me put another unpalatable thought to you: imperialism
led to evil, but, though we may believe in the socialist ethic of
cooperation, yet we may have to recognise that Western
European Capitalism has, so far, given greater happiness to
greater numbers than Soviet Socialism appears to have done.

That's not easy for someone of the Left (like myself) to
explain away. Qualifying observations are possible and necessary
but not easy to form. For example: we know it's true that
Western European Capitalism achieved its liberal nature under
pressure from Socialist thinkers and agitators — but is it enough
to say just that? Capitalism has been around long enough for us
to recognise its internal contradictions; but is Socialism without
its own internal contradictions? And perhaps common to both
in creating those contradictions is the nature and condition of
human beings whose unpredictability, mixed appetites and
diverse motives will always create contradictions, whatever the
society which produces them.

Therefore shouldn't the understanding of that 'human
condition' be of paramount importance? Isn't it the teacher who,

from our early years, with the aid of what has been written by many thoughtful individuals, must help us to measure carefully what in human nature may be called evil? And isn't it the 'poet', the one who cherishes the precise value and weight in the meaning of each word? Isn't he or she the thoughtful one who should be trusted to name what in human nature really merits the description of evil? Between the teacher and the artist, cannot an awareness of those contradictions be communicated, illustrated, and, if not resolved, at least debated in a way that might lessen their tensions? Is there such a subject on any school curriculum: 'Human Nature'? The 'Human Condition'?

We'll come back to the school curriculum in a moment, let's now return to words. Corruption and authoritarianism may lead to evil, but they are not the same beasts; and it's important to be absolutely clear that they're not the same beast, because evil may finally demand arms to destroy it, but corruption and intransigent authority should perhaps be met by the tried processes of argument and legislation. The bullet may be a short cut for short tempers, but blood is too precious to sacrifice at the altar of impatience and lazy definitions. Evil is a word describing something very awful and therefore must be carefully measured and accurately named, because the gun is a dangerous weapon and the world a complex place; neither charge of the gun nor understanding of the world should be given to unsubtle minds.

Ah! Unsubtle minds! Am I suggesting that the task of developing the subtle mind should be based upon a special school project? Yes, just that! Also, that such a subject should have to do with 'human nature' and be understood through language, and that this task should be given to the teacher who must use the arts to illustrate his new subject. To me, as a Socialist, if education means anything it means essentially this: the upholding of language as man's greatest creation. It means a constant freshening, a constant guarding against abuse by demagogues, bureaucrats and copy-writers, whether political or commercial.

The Artist

People have been starving, suffering and fighting tyrants and one another since the beginning of time, their energies constantly absorbed by mere existence, only rarely having sufficient peace to pause and consider the next stage after securing existence: securing happiness and fulfilment.

We always seem forced to concentrate our energies upon coping with the miseries caused by the tyrant and never get to asking the question how did he get there in the first place? The result usually is that we're led to destroy one tyrant with another embryo tyrant at our head. Demagogues lead us to fight demagogues, not to free us but simply to take over. Bellies have always needed to be filled (I do not say 'always will'), and so, in addition to other enormous problems, the simple question: 'Why have men persistently allowed tyrants into their midst or demagogues to turn them against one another?' goes unanswered, except among a few tiresome artists, unreadable philosophers, and weary, embattled academics.

Worse! Not only are human problems enormous but those weary artists and intellectuals, who know in very vivid ways how enormous the problems are, are not taken any notice of anyway! And demagogical, or authoritarian political leaders, whether in power or aspiring to power, have good reason to feel safe in not taking any notice of them. It has always been a simple task persuading society to denigrate its artists, and view the teacher as a mere aid to passing examinations. So well has it been done in the West that the artist, for example, has been coerced into denigrating his own powers and dignity. 'Why!' he cries in spiritual self-flagellation, diminishing his role like an old-fashioned sinner, 'what *is* an artist anyway? All people are artists!' (Thus, by the way, making it easy for himself if, by chance, it is discovered he has no real talent!) Or, he says, guiltily, 'Why should my pictures of the human condition be more valid than another's?' the presumption of his calling having been made more than he can bear.

Guilts for the presumption of art! How cleverly that argument has been used to reduce the artist to an impotent, apologetic thing, easy to lose, fatten, and confuse with flattery. Yet it's an argument to be faced and demolished, for it *is* true — artists *do* presume. Constantly. But don't we all? For each other? Personally I don't mind presumption in others —

especially those to do with art, which presume I might be moved by the revelations in this woman's novel, the questioning spirit of that man's poem, another's interpretation of world events.

Yet others are *encouraged* to mind such presumptions. It seems as though politicians — or commercial entrepreneurs with huge profits to earn — anxious about the revelatory nature of art and the questioning spirit engendered by the artist, seek to divert both revelation and question by perpetrating the myth that all art is an imposition, a presumption. Some artists, terrified of such accusations, have been known to race apologetically to the other extreme and declare that all art is Fascist, since it *dictates* a view of the world on a captive audience — I've heard that applied to the theatre. It's of course an absurdly perverse definition of the process of art, and one that I believe has been cleverly insinuated into the consciousness of societies all around the world by those who fear the revelatory and questioning qualities of art; those revelatory qualities which identify the embryo tyrant, or question the demagogue, or delineate the evils or absurdities in our society, which reveal the devil in the making — whether it's the political devil or the private one within us.

But let's assume the artist's presumptions are tolerated. (The demagogue can take that in his stride!) The artist is still not content. He not only knows the problems are enormous but more — he knows the problems are endless! He is incorrigible, this artist. Built into a philosophy of society (he says) must be both the awareness that the problems are endless and the provision of machinery to cope with it. Having located a problem (he says) it is society's responsibility not merely to look for a solution and then impose it, but to be prepared to recognise that by the time the solution is ready, the nature of the problem may have altered, or that the chemical reaction of the solution applied to the problem may produce another problem. Because (says our irritating artist) we need to remember that, when either occurs, then the men and women trained to think and apply their solutions may be absurd people, or people deformed by vanities or stultified by unsubtle minds, which will prevent their conceding mistakes and changing course, and there! *there's* the rub!

When all our blueprints are mapped out, then people —
poor, vulnerable, soured and tired men and women, with
perhaps unhappy lives — must apply them; and who knows into
what unimaginative, crude hands the beautiful dreams will fall.
What a Marx may dream a Stalin may be left to enact. Or, not
to take easy examples, what an enlightened minister of social
services conceives, a bitter official behind the counter of the
local office for social services is left to apply! Or, even more
difficult perhaps, what an experienced worker in the office
for social services understands *should* happen, a blind or
stubborn minister ignores.

No one is safe from such weapons. The artist will be
outraged by not merely the tyrant — which is easy, but by the
Socialist petty official — which is difficult because once you're
a socialist official, you represent the will of the people which
few dare question. The artist is outraged not merely by the
cruelty of Fascism, which is easy, but by the unhealthy envies
and spites of left-wing or religious fanatics, which is not so
easy because they can hide behind lofty ideology. Not even
close friends can trust the artist not to reveal their absurdities,
or embarrass them with his own. The 'poet' is an uncomfortable
member of a community's team.

Now, one more loose end. The last war produced a
monstrous state crime: the decision to exterminate 'inferior'
people was elevated to a carefully defined philosophy that
men seriously considered, then accepted, and then executed
in the form of gas chambers. This was an evil unprecedented
in that it was not a massacre in pursuit of gain, or to revenge
a wrong — it was none of the normal warring between equal,
although idiotic, combatants. No, it was the gracing of
barbarism with *justification by language.* Language was perverted
to such a degree that it became possible to persuade men not
simply that they were superior, but also that others whom they
considered as *not* superior should be exterminated. Dr. George
Steiner and others have written on this with much greater
erudition than I could possibly muster. The value of this
article, if it has a value, is not to compete with their study of
the complex relations between language and political inhumanity.
No, this article is a simple leading-up to one simple suggestion.

Simple, that is, to articulate — not to operate.

Let me remind you that I'm arguing for a place of high priority in society for the artist and teacher. How, to recapitulate simply, do we use their special gifts to help create a civilised, articulate, thoughtful and wise community of men and women who know when they need leaders, who know how to choose them, and who know when to change them; and who know this to such a degree that they are left the energy for, what many believe is our real purpose, the discovery and fulfilment of all that is within us to be useful, to do good, to give pleasure, and to satisfy our own spiritual and physical needs? A community of people with those subtle minds! These are my suggestions:

The Suggestion

It is my view — and an extreme one, I grant you — that education means absolutely nothing unless the implications of the gas chambers of Nazi Germany are constantly presented to the consciousness of the pupil. What happened to language in Germany that it 'allowed' itself to be the carrier of such inhumane concepts? Is the same happening to language today? Nor does the holocaust hold lessons only for language: alongside it should be measured history, science, literature, politics.*

But, how do you do this? How does my son know whether the punch in the eye was a mere casual act of thuggery, or whether resentments were at work there which neither the bullies nor my son understood? How do youngsters measure their experience? What (and this is fundamental) has education formulated to enable such measurements to be made? There is

---

* 'There are other questions, difficult to answer. How much of what happened should be made known to serve as a warning and a deterrent, and how little so as not to become absorbed into our everyday culture? How much knowledge is necessary to avoid the Holocaust being considered as merely a unique fluke in history, and how little so as not to desensitize the human senses about the acts of barbarism committed in *l'univers concentrationnaire*?'
Vera Elyashiv reviewing Holocaust literature in *The Jewish Quarterly* Vol. 24 No.1/2

a great deal more that children experience from, or do to, each other — which is the basis for what adults experience from, and do to, each other — that is not understood by the child. Is there in a school curriculum anywhere in the world a subject that handles — human nature? What shall we call such a subject? Definitions of experience? What words are being assembled over six years in school which might illuminate history's massacres and thumps in the eye for the child? What might help my son, or any child, to recognize the causes and signs of disorder, so that evils may be averted rather than acted out?

From these questions follows my suggestion, which is in two parts. Part one: the creation of a new school subject which should be called 'definitions of experience'. Part two: the creation of a primary vocabulary to help define experience.

Let me illustrate this. Take a word like 'intimidate'. Intimidation describes a sensation some people feel, and a behaviour others enact. And the fear, unease, confusion *felt* by the one, and the menace, distress, insecurity *caused* by the other, must surely be among the most basic of experiences which people meet in their everyday relationships one to another. Now, is there a moment in any school where an imaginative, fully trained teacher takes that word in front of a class and shakes it inside out for its meaning, for its appearance in the contemporary world, in history, or — most important — for application to the pupil's own life? I'm not talking about a half an hour devoted to discussing the meaning of the word. Nor of a lesson. But of perhaps a whole month, two lessons a week. Eight sessions devoted to one word, and using for illustration the rich fields of painting, literature, and film. At the end of the first year: eight words. At the end of six years: nearly fifty words.

Words! Vindictive. Lilliputian. Mockery. Superficial. Spurious. Greed. Relativity. Tolerance. Doubt. Reason. Faith. Freedom. Demagogue . . . A linguistic survival kit!

It's not simply a question of building up a vocabulary about which the child may boast but of fitting together the jigsaw of experience, of building a battery of concepts. I don't know what those words should be. Individuals with other qualifications could list such an initial vocabulary for understanding the human condition. I do not say guaranteeing an understanding of the human condition. Nothing can guarantee that! But a basis, upon which there exists a possibility for understanding. That basis, that 'beginner's kit' must be possible to evolve. Men and women have built essential words over centuries, giving names to their actions and sensations, pinning them down for all time. And when once a word was found inadequate, another was found to describe the nuance.

There's the challenge! How many words belong to such a basic list? Is it fifty? A hundred? And what would they be? What would be the first dozen words you'd want your child to understand?

I may not possess the qualifications to reason it through and end up with such a list as I'm suggesting exists — nor would this be the place to do so. But it is perhaps incumbent upon me to indicate how thinking about such a list might have to begin.

For instance, since I'm talking about words which contain within them concepts affecting human behaviour, rather than words which describe human behaviour, then the concept of 'morality' is of more value in this basic vocabulary than the descriptive force of the word 'cretin'; just as the more seminal concept of 'conscience' is of more value than the more minor concept of 'irony'. Or *is* irony a minor concept? Is the concept of life as being frequently the bitter opposite of its promise sufficiently fundamental to include in our basic vocabulary?

And where does one start? What should be the first word? Since we are dealing with words as concepts then should the word 'concept' be the very first word we struggle to make the eleven-year-old child comprehend? Is the eleven-year-old mind able to comprehend such an abstract concept as 'conceptualising'? I'm not qualified to answer that with confidence; but I would have thought that — as an example — the freedom to follow one's own individual conscience is a concept that can be illustrated from much in literature. Some illustrations? Take Ibsen's *An Enemy of the People*; or the film, *On the Waterfront*; or in history, the story of Luther; and in contemporary life, the trade-union closed-shop disputes; and from science, the story of Galileo.

But what word follows the word 'concept'? After eight lessons aiming to fix in the child's mind the process of conceptualising, what does one then offer? Perhaps, in the next two months, two of the most fundamental concepts to all human activity — the concepts of freedom and of responsibility?

That would seem a good next two month's work. But — can the child be expected to understand the concepts of freedom and responsibility without first having an understanding of the concept of morality — which concept carries with it the need to make distinctions between good and evil? How can youngsters be expected to grasp — as they'd have to — that freedom has necessary limitations, if they haven't grasped the need to distinguish between good and evil?

From which, one is forced to ask: shouldn't the concept of 'relative' (or 'relativity') be offered to the child for consideration before asking him to grapple with the concepts of freedom, responsibility and morality? Because freedom of speech may be an *absolute* good which we all desire, but not *all* things are absolutely good — some, like pamphlets on language, are only relatively good! In fact, since most things are relative, perhaps *that* should be the second concept to follow the word 'concept'?

Or perhaps — and this is the last mind-bender I will offer — before even the word 'concept' should be the word 'reason'. There is a very good argument to be made for implanting, before anything else, a sound understanding of the concept of 'to reason'; for 'to reason' is to think logically, consecutively, to deduce one thing from another, to use the mind in order to arrive at an understanding of something, rather than to act blindly and thoughtlessly.

Now, should it be thought that my only concern is for language, for its ethical qualities, or its ability to handle ethical considerations, let me add very briefly that, though I consider an understanding of language an essential prerequisite for an 'ethically' just society, yet of equal importance are the *imaginative* qualities of language and the ability of language to stimulate the imagination. And for that reason, words such as 'imagination' and 'poetry', 'dialogue' and 'culture' would be part of *my* basic vocabulary. 'Dialogue' to engender the habit of imaginatively placing one's self in another person's position; and 'culture' as an umbrella word under which the child would be made conscious of the thrillingly wide range of human activity — the arts, crafts, industry, traditions and social habits of different ethnic groups.

You will see now why this is not the place to work out such a vocabulary, even were I equipped to do so. But I hope I've indicated the principle which ought perhaps to guide its formation. Can 'freedom' be understood without first understanding 'morality'; or 'morality' be adequately grasped before considering 'relativity'; or either of these three before being aware of the nature of 'the concept'; or does comprehending any of these words rest primarily upon a vivid understanding of the process of 'reasoning'? Which word must come before another in such a vocabulary? That's the nature and scope of the challenge.

And, finally, to bring us back to the beginning again: would discussion of the word 'intimidate' in my son's school have made him understand that it was not the thug intimidating him, but he — with his long hair, colourful clothing, disregard for the school uniform, extensive vocabulary, his entire personality and output of confidence — it was *he* who was intimidating the thug. Such understanding of the word 'intimidation' can't keep a swelling down; but it might have prompted him to move on at the first sign of danger, or to have faced it squarely to show he was going to hit back.

It has been said before by persons of authority: language is our most precious instrument. Despite abuse and all that has been done to language and committed in its name, it is the most extraordinary piece of equipment forged by men and women for their better understanding of themselves, one another, and the world in which they live. Words describe and give names to what men feel, think, see, and do; and so command of them is of paramount importance. And yet, nowhere that I know of is their importance sufficiently appreciated for them to be — in some form or other, with a title like 'definitions of experience' — number one subject on the curriculum.

Is it any wonder that time and time again people can be persuaded to commit acts of brutality against one another? Or that they can be led to pursue policies which history has repeatedly proven fruitless? No one has taught them to identify rhetoric and its dangers.

Yes, I know, perhaps it is history that should have a greater prominence on the school curriculum. But the *facts* of history especially require a conceptual understanding of words before their lessons can be interpreted — and then learned.

I know that I'm defending words as though they were the only form of language. Of course I know that some experience, some feelings, some of what we see and think cannot be put into the language of words. And so man, incredible man, made other languages for himself: music, painting, sculpture. But though visual, musical, as well as verbal, languages are crucial as a basis for developing sensitivities, perceptions and critical judgements, yet it can't be denied that the language of words is that most commonly used and therefore requires a special attention.

Panaceas, we've long agreed, there are none. Guarantees for civilised behaviour neither. Two acts can be expected of people: that they survive first, and then, if they can survive, that they be brotherly. Helping the young to identify, locate, define what's happening to them and what they're doing to other people must surely contribute to a basic arsenal for survival and fraternity.

London
19 September 1975
First delivered as a lecture in Italy for the A.C.I.

FINDING ONE'S OWN VOICE

an afterword on Wesker's WORDS and his plays
with reference to the educational theory of Paulo Freire

Richard Appignanesi

Critical Publishing

Publishers publish. Writers write. Readers read.

Neat categories! And what could be more obvious? Or you could scramble them a bit and say, readers sometimes write, publishers sometimes read, etc. But then you would miss reflecting upon two things which that fixed order suggests.

What *do* these two-word sentences assert?

I am not being whimsical if I single out a descending order of control over the production, creation and diffusion of books. To get the full weight of the implied hierarchy, try re-reading those assertive sentences as ones of command. Publishers, publish! Writers, write! etc. Everyone knows that, in the normal course of things, readers have less control over what writers do than writers. But writers have less control over what *they* do than publishers. To be fair, I should complete this not very startling revelation by adding — and accountants (the grey eminences of the profit-motive) have more control over publishers than is usually admitted. Book-keeping, not books, is finally what matters. Alas!

The second point is that the activities — publishing, writing and reading — are very separate indeed. Or to put it another way, one should say separateness permits very little *intervention* from the broad base of readers upwards. Here I employ Freire's terminology of cultural criticism. What does this mean? Simply, intervention from the base upwards means readers *asking* for the books they need; but, as things now go, there is very little chance of readers being in the *position* to ask. Market-researchers can scurry round and do the asking: 'What do you need? We'll supply it!' That's not intervention but interference from the top again. Paulo Freire has a better name for such typical interference based on the relationships of authority — 'cultural invasion'.

> The invader thinks, at most, *about* the invaded, never *with* them; the latter have their thinking done for them by the former. The invader dictates; the invaded patiently accept what is dictated.[1]

Readers won't ask unless they grow aware of their own needs. While awareness won't be encouraged no matter how many tons of books are dropped down the abstract flue of supply-and-demand. This holds true as much for the tonnage of cookery and gardening books as for the books on or about or by Marx or any other writer. (This should put paid to that age-old, philistine remark, 'But books have never stopped wars!' Such remarks are not intended to be useful or critical. On the contrary, their aim is to sabotage critical thought by 'poisoning the wells'. If one reflects on the sheer disproportion between the numbers of books produced and the tiny, fragmented state of their reception, there is hardly any cause to wonder except at the social barriers which so long prevented access to reading. How many people were *able* to read — let alone *ask* for books to stop wars?)

Reaching people only goes half way towards effective publishing. Publishers may promote all they like; but they cannot finally expect to teach people to ask. That's the job of educators, and, even then, effective only within the context of radical social action.

So then, — what are the reasons for publishing this little pamphlet, which Wesker himself admits is 'simple, rudimentary'?

Publishers like ourselves who claim to publish on principle; who claim to seek unconventional channels of diffusion, should reserve a little energy to elucidate the logic behind their programme. Every now and again, we ought to tell readers where we are, why and what we do. This shouldn't mean that we issue barrel-thumping or self-congratulatory manifestos. We could opt to say nothing — and just hope for adventurous (but anonymous) readers. We could adopt the shield of anonymity which the three commands, publish, write, read, pretty well guarantee. But if we take seriously the task of being critical publishers, we have to admit to ourselves and to others that the book — the finished book which goes on the market — is not often enough the common ground on which readers, writers and publishers really meet. Not anything like it! Separateness, anonymity, dissociation of function: these social phenomena create a very odd situation in which books come into existence apparently without direction.

Very well. Let's consider for a moment the Cooperative's education list, so that some sense can be made of Arnold Wesker's potential contribution to it.

Here, as in other areas, we try to follow a logic, and not
just produce books helter-skelter, lumping them together under
that catch-all catalogue term, 'education'. Some two years ago,
we began publishing with a single, very short, very cheaply
priced pamphlet, Ivan Illich's 'After Deschooling What?' Since
then we have added two more pamphlets on the literacy process;
and, at the same time, key critical texts published by others were
promoted by means of our direct mail-order system. Now we
have re-issued a major theoretical work, Paulo Freire's
'Education: The Practice of Freedom'. Other books will follow;
but this is so far not a large list. Yet, while this reflects our
modest economic capacities, we would not wish to move a great
deal faster. Why? Two reasons.

We don't pretend to be unique in being the first to publish
important or radical education thinkers. Our intention instead
is very carefully to select radical works and issue them on the
basis of length, and cheap selling price, so as to stress their
availability. But, more important, we wish to issue them at a
rhythm which encourages readership response:-a time to think,
to ask, to become aware . . . and I don't only mean readers but
we ourselves, the publishers! The point is not merely to create
a list with a 'partisan' identity, but to add slowly, deliberately
to what people can *identify with.* Our programme moves ahead
at a speed no greater than our own understanding of cooperative
relations (which includes understanding economic relations too).
It takes time — time to think, to ask and to become aware —
to reforge the broken, sometimes non-existent links of dialogue
between publisher, writer and reader. But that is our slow,
deliberate plan.

'How nice,' a sceptic may say balefully. 'But it sounds
romantic, your business of identifying with, dialogue,
cooperation. What does it mean practically?'

Yes, practically. — It is surprisingly practical. Consider that
as a group we have grown into publishers from a non-professional
status and with very little money. Our identification with
'writers and readers' is not an ideological reflection but a fact.[2]

Consider another point. There are some two million
functionally illiterate adults in England and Wales. Very few

when compared to the vast numbers of illiterates in the so-called Third World. This is not the place to offer criticisms of UNESCO's programme or our own government's plans to remedy illiteracy. But let me quote the following from a work which treats the question more fully:

> Throughout a diversity of situations the aim of functional literacy remains basically the same: to mobilize, train and educate still insufficiently utilized manpower to make it more productive. The ideology behind many literacy programmes is to accelerate the adult so that he produces more, succeeds better, and thereby contributes to the economic development of his country. In this process he will become a 'better worker and in fact a better "man".'[3]

This quotation implies that illiteracy *and* literacy both hav political, socio-cultural and historical dimensions. Illiteracy cannot be separated off and 'treated' as a marginal dys-function. It is a reality with much deeper social implications than the 'functional' inability to read and write. People reduced to the condition of mutes, partly through illiteracy, form what Freire defines as the 'culture of silence'.

> In the culture of silence the masses are 'mute', that is, they are prohibited from creatively taking part in the transformation of their society and therefore prohibited from being. Even if they can occasionally read and write because they were 'taught' in humanitarian — but not humanist — literacy campaigns, they are nevertheless alienated from the power responsible for their silence.[4]

Illiterates, Freire says, are dominated, castrated in their right to transform the world. Yet, others who can read, who can write, do not necessarily begin transforming their world either. Theirs is a marginal literacy which permits them to 'function' as economic contributors; but, to use Freire's terminology again, they haven't experienced *cultural literacy* which liberates rather than dominates human beings. Note here: when I say 'can read, can write', I don't only have in mind culturally disadvantaged people. I include also the apparently privileged — even writers. Writers whose 'function' within the cultural apparatus is one more of frail status than relevance; whose real place within the establishment is anything but secure. (Very few writers are Arthur Hailey or Harold Robbins . . . or even Graham

Greene. And this says nothing about the scores of poets, non-fiction writers, journalists, etc.)

I don't say we offer them, or anyone else, some kind of transcendental solution. No one can 'offer' action. What we can do, however, is give currency to the active, problem-posing nature of cultural literacy which regards dialogue 'as indispensable to the act of cognition which unveils reality.'[5]

Fine. But concretely? Practically? How begin the terrifically hard job of creating cooperative links between publishing, writing and reading?

Allow me to cite one more example from our publishing programme. We have published critical papers on children's literature. These papers represent a certain consciousness of certain problems relating to race, class and sex. They were written by people in community-based groups, and, as such, in whatever small way, they voice readership awareness. Questions are asked by readers *as social beings* about the content of children's literature. Practice, and indeed common sense and logic, demand that such criticism be absorbed into actual children's books. Someone should produce the 'real' thing which critical readers ask for. We have now published such books. Even more logically, these are specially designed children's books which have absorbed Elena Belotti's criticism of sex-role stereotyping in her book, 'Little Girls', another one of our publications.

The logic should be clear. We try to follow up critical, problem-posing works, those 'indispensable to the act of cognition which unveils reality', with others which come still closer to practice (usefulness-in-action).

The presence of critical education theory doesn't solve the problem of its application. The teacher, in the practical circumstances of the classroom, may be hard pressed to discover links with the local situation in Britain which Freire's work among Brazilian slum-dwellers does not supply. There have to be home-grown examples: illustrative practice rooted in the 'unveiled reality' of our own culture here and now.

Chris Searle's 'Classrooms of Resistance' goes some way towards supplying a mode of specific, illustrative practice, of 'teaching English' as an extension of cultural literacy. We need more local texts of this kind. And, finally, this brings me to Arnold Wesker's present essay, *Words as Definitions of Experience.*

He asks: 'Is there in the curriculum of any school anywhere in the world a subject which handles — *the human condition?* Is there an education programme anywhere which provides children with a basic survival-kit of language?' He asks for, 1) 'a new school subject which should be called "definitions of experience",' and 2) 'the creation of a primary vocabulary to help define experience.'

Wesker is one of Britain's best-known dramatists. He writes plays. He is not a pedagogical expert, theoretician or teacher. He offers the views of *a writer,* not magical prescriptions. 'My concern,' Wesker says, 'is to defend language as a means of both naming and comprehending the implications of the experience of *what is being done to one, and what one is doing to others.'* Implications which are precisely those of 'drama'. Indeed, he recommends that anyone teaching this specially set-aside subject could draw upon works of literature, art and film to illustrate key conceptual words, and so build up the young person's basic survival-kit.

'But' — I can hear someone object — 'by what right can a writer of fiction *presume* to speak on education? Isn't this better left to specialists?'

My reply to that — and the Cooperative's — is: if we left things to specialists, we wouldn't be publishing! Our arguments against separateness of function are meant seriously. 'Specialism' can so easily lead to cultural inequity. It can contribute to what Freire calls cultural invasion — the silencing of 'askers' by diminishing them to the level of in-expertness. Besides, Wesker himself confronts this accusation of so-called artistic 'presumption' in his essay. Brief as his remarks are, they suffice to raise the question (and a bedevilled one it is too) of the unrealized social potential which resides in literature; of its rich vein of typified experience which has never really been mined at all.

Our intellectual elite has long been guilty of shunning this problem — worse, of diminishing it. The dead hand of formalistic irony stretches all the way from the highest of

highbrow academics down to meanest of mean reviewers.
'Irony-mongers' they ought to be called; and formalists because
they separate art off as something closed, suspended in a 'form'
of specialized relevance which is, in a word, too *distant* to
matter. There it hangs — the fruit of experts! Dare we eat of it?
Or will it turn to ashes at a touch? . . . Or is it poisoned?
Because, correctly, Wesker says there is a notion of literature
about which quite consciously intends to intimidate. Influential
irony which poisons. In fact, Wesker does ask whether the word
'irony' should have a place in the young person's kit.

> Or *is* 'irony' a minor concept? Is the concept of life as being
> frequently the bitter opposite of its promise sufficiently
> fundamental to include in our basic vocabulary?

Good question!

Someone else might object, 'But, look here. Don't schools
already have English courses? Why burden students with a new
subject (which sounds very like grammar or something)?'

Replying to this, if I may do so in Wesker's stead, I would
say that the aim of WORDS as a new school subject is different.
Simply, the point is to get at the *experience,* the concepts of
human behaviour, embedded in language: and by means of
illustrative teaching — through discussion, through dialogue —
awaken minds to what lies dormant or unconscious in words
of key significance. This way, insight-learning is acquired, which
differs radically from implanting information through
conditioning. Kohler, a German psychologist, calls such
insight-learning the *Aha-Erlebnis* or Aha! Experience. This, as
its colourful name suggests, is an illuminative capacity to solve
problems which is released in humans as well as animals.

> Knowledge acquired through this kind of learning process tends
> to be 'internalized' in such a way that it can be used in solving
> many different and unfamiliar problems a long time after the
> actual moment of learning. 'Insight' learning experiences are also
> known gradually and spontaneously to integrate with other
> knowledge experiences learnt by the same method.[6]

The long-term result is that young people mature rationally
They will be enabled, now and in adulthood too, to confront
tense or explosive situations with insight. They will be able to

say, 'That's a good question! Let's discuss it.' Rather than, 'You bastard! I'll kill you!' Potentially harmful, irrational reactions are re-routed towards harmless, but at the same time, useful thought.

To grasp the difference between WORDS and any set English course, one has to understand the stress placed on experience of language use. For this, even parts of literary works, and not necessarily the whole of any one, might be found useful. The choice rests with the individual teacher's wit and ingenuity, since it is the constellation of primary words rather than a set literature programme which will count. Wesker does not say his suggestions constitute a system, complete and ready to use. Others, better equipped than he by experience must think deeply before coming up with the Aha! which will illuminate a genuinely practical method.

To make a little clearer what I mean by employing parts of literary works, let me give some examples. Let's say that the word 'intimidate' were included in our survival-kit, as Wesker suggests. Let's say, too, that we had moved on in our discussion of that word to specific experiential instances of it. That we wished, say, to study the question I had raised earlier on — of cultural intimidation which has a distancing effect; which makes people feel remote from 'higher things' and impotent in regard to them. Someone wishing to illustrate this problem could do worse than start with one of Wesker's own plays, *Roots,* and particularly its final climactic speeches.

' . . . I'm like you. Stubborn, empty, wi' no tools for livin'.' Those who have seen — or read — Wesker's *Roots* will remember the despairing cry of that play's heroine, Beatie Bryant. Slapped only moments ago by her mother, Beatie exclaims, 'I got no roots in nothing. I come from a family o' farm labourers yet I ent got no roots — just like town people — just a mass o' nothin'.'

'You got a family ent you?' Beatie's father reminds her. Yes. But that doesn't take the sting out of the slap; or, far worse, the taunt which accompanies it. Pent-up resentment makes Beatie's mother shrewd, and she says, with every intention of wounding her daughter, ' . . . she go away from here and fill her head wi' high-class squit and then it turn out she don't understand any on it herself. It turn out she do just the same things she say I do.'

How many working class youngsters have heard that tune before! ' . . . the apple don't fall far from the tree do it?'

Here, in the closing minutes of the play, Wesker vividly, realistically dramatizes what Freire calls the 'culture of silence'. Particularly those ambiguities, those inner divisions which add to the afflictions of the disadvantaged.

So, for instance, Beatie's mother orders her, 'Go on, Lady Nevershit — talk, if you're so smart!' while at the same time inhibiting any possible reply with a contradictory jeer, 'We don't know what you're on about!'

Beatie's mother uses irony — the heavy-handed sort, of course, not the highbrow influential kind. Yet, similar enough, so that she imitates the oppressor while remaining herself oppressed. Freire describes this internal contradiction within the unfree:

> The oppressed suffer from the duality which has established itself in their innermost being. They discover that without freedom they cannot exist authentically. Yet, although they desire authentic existence, they fear it. They are at one and the same time themselves and the oppressor whose consciousness they have internalized.[7]

Freire poses the problem in theoretical terms. Wesker shows us the *lived-in* experience. Certainly, one could study the whole play, as is in fact done in English drama courses. But the last pages of *Roots* contain enough substance to illustrate a particular sub-species of intimidation. Something important happens to Beatie Bryant. She *does* begin to talk. She finds her own voice. Or, more exactly, she begins to articulate the divisions within her own being, as though the fragmented parts of herself, silenced till now, began arguing one against the other. Silence gives way to painful healing. 'Well, am I right?' Beatie finally asks. 'You know I'm right.' She is appealing as much to herself as to the others — the oppressed appealing to the oppressed.

> Education ent only books and music — it's asking questions, all the time. There are millions of us, all over the country, and no one, not one of us, is asking questions, we're all taking the easiest way out. Everyone I ever worked with took the easiest

way out. We don't fight for anything, we're so mentally lazy we might as well be dead. Blust, we are dead!

When the unfree finally awaken, Freire says

. . . their struggle for freedom threatens not only the oppressor, but also their own oppressed comrades who are fearful of still greater repression. When they discover in themselves the yearning to be free, they perceive that this yearning can be transformed into reality only when the same yearning is aroused in their comrades.[8]

Beatie knows very well the wretched self-accusation of the deprived — 'art is not for us'. She knows it because she's said it to herself, 'art ent for *me*.' But because she is not 'outside' that self-accusation, she also knows its double meaning. Others, depending on theory, need careful listening to catch the double-bind — the Catch 22. Not Beatie! *art is not for us* . . . There is resignation in that; defeat in the face of what is 'higher', 'better'. But — and a crucial but — there is also refusal, aroused resentment. Beatie's family turn against her. She is the uprooted renegade, and they . . . well, *they* have the 'just as good' alternative; the traditional 'us against 'em.' Gregariousness passes for genuine class solidarity. Beatie knows this deeply. 'But *us* count?' she says, and so argues as if against her own double. 'I wonder. Do we? Do you think we really count?'

You don' wanna take any notice of what them ole papers say about the workers bein' all-important these days — that's all squit! 'Cos we aren't. Do you think when the really talented people in the country get to work they get to work for us? Hell if they do! Do you think they don't know we 'ont make the effort? The writers don't write thinkin' we can understand, nor the painters don't paint expecting us to be interested — that they don't, nor don't the composers give out music thinking we can appreciate it. 'Blust,' they say, 'the masses is too stupid for us to come down to them. Blust,' they say, 'if they don't make no effort why should we bother?' So you know who come along? The slop singers and the pop writers and the film makers and women's magazines and the Sunday papers and the picture strip love stories — that's who come along, and you don't have to make no effort for them, it come easy. 'We know where the money lie,' they say, 'hell we do! The workers've got it so let's give them what they want. If they want slop songs and film idols we'll give 'em that then.

If they want words of one syllable, we'll give 'em that then.
If they want the third-rate, *blust!* We'll give 'em *that* then.
Anything's good enough for them 'cos they don't ask for no
more!' The whole stinkin' commercial world insults us and we
don't care a damn.

Thus, as the play ends, Beatie finds her own voice, while
paying the penalty of not being heard by her own family. Is
that irony? Defeat? The objection is often made against art
that it over-stresses individual salvation at the expense of
society. Wesker dramatizes a true, familiar experience of
isolation. It would be wrong-headed to say, 'Beatie is talking
about something *she* needs but they don't,' because this
familiar objection itself succumbs unconsciously to elite irony
and intimidation. Such irony also isolates. Rather than slide
easily into intellectual treason, one should ask, 'What has
Beatie learnt?' What is the positive, dynamic alternative to
intimidation? What does her individual learning-experience
contribute to the *whole* picture?

Existential experience is a whole (Freire says). In illuminating
one of its angles and perceiving the interrelation between
that angle and others, the learners tend to replace a fragmented
vision of reality with a total vision.[9]

I think one can begin to see the potential of the subject
Wesker pleads for. The development of the young person's
conceptual vocabulary would draw widely — from literature,
from social history and even science and philosophy. But it
would do so by translating these 'separate' studies into the
experience of language use.

Now, I would like to consider some aspects of Wesker's
work which suggest that his preoccupation with 'words' depends
upon his outlook and commitment as a writer.

Labour, Beauty, Reason . . . and Defending Language

Three features distinguish Wesker's plays from those by other
contemporary British playwrights. One can single them out and
perhaps name them (as I do) preoccupations with labour, beauty
and reason. Or call them themes, if you prefer, or elements
recurring often enough to mark Wesker as a socialist writer —

indeed, of a 'classic' type.

Take the first most striking feature — labour. Wesker is one of the very few dramatists who dramatizes work. Think of *The Kitchen* or *Their Very Own And Golden City* or more recently still *The Journalists*. People in Wesker's plays are always busy doing something — working or planning or building. One gets a real sense of work rhythms: of physical activity striving to fill — and fulfill — space. This is not an empty symbol or some kind of 'work ethic'. Work is people becoming. There you have the first principle of socialism, one which has often and variously been re-stated: for instance — social relations are extensions of the labour process. One could express that less coldly as commitment to the principle of Hope. And *that* is the sense of the activity in Wesker's plays. Human beings are *un-completed,* unfinished. They don't only produce objects but also themselves — their nature as human beings, their culture as social beings. They gaze ahead. Hope is revolutionary futurity.[10]

Equally important in Wesker's plays is the emphasis on 'good things'. Good tasty food. Beautifully-crafted furniture. Good books. Good buildings to live in. Beautiful things, yes, an environment of beauty. That springs naturally, logically from a socialist conviction about the *incompleteness* of our social life, and which again implies gazing ahead hopefully.

Of course, everyone wants 'good things'. But beauty in everyday life too frequently appears under the exceptional guise of luxury. Luxury is the boundary of privilege. Too much for too few. What will secure us beauty as a reflection of life? Whither? When? How? Good things are questions. In this sense, beauty is criticism — criticism of the limits of our own capitalist society and of the shortcomings of socialist society too. We may work to produce abundance; but without the surplus exuberance of beauty we fail.

'Good things' may be said to serve as Utopian image, as revolutionary future, as a promise of a vastly more satisfying life. But good things alone cannot shore up enough reassurance against spiritual vacuity. *Intellectual incompleteness.* Emptiness. Emptiness which breeds intimidation and social violence. Emptiness as much of countless empty stomachs as of empty minds. With *what* can we fight injustice (which is at bottom privilege reinforced by corruption and stupidity)? With violence? Sometimes, yes. But with reason, always. Violence provides the short-term answer to violence. But it doesn't guarantee social improvement. Sooner or later the harder, frustrating, unglamorous task of education will have to be faced. Only a genuine programme of education will begin radically to change people — or to use the critical term, 'de-alienate' them.

I don't wish to reduce Wesker's plays to a 'message'; but, without crude distortion, one recognizes that he has been saying something like this all along. Labour, beauty . . . and reason. Wesker's insistence on rational means to combat oppression. Reason — and *words*. Effective language. Language as a critical instrument of reason. Strong, clear, polemical and passionate words. What else do we have? What else can express? Can guide? So it is hardly a surprise that Wesker pleads for a survival-kit of words.

Sceptics will again object: 'Expression? Do you think that's enough to confront the *inexpressible* depths of injustice, of violence and evil in this world? Is reason enough?'

What else *do* we have? Can we afford anything besides reason to combat irrationality? Right language guides right action.

> Human existence cannot be silent, nor can it be nourished by false words, but only by true words, with which men transform the world. To exist, humanly, is to *name* the world, to change it.[11]

Wesker dramatizes reason, just as he does labour and beauty. He is one of the very few — and maybe one of the last — rational writers. A writer with a rational vision. But why 'rational'? By that, I mean his relation to language: the use the characters in his plays *make* of words. Every writer works with (and on) words — granted. Granted too — every writer has a peculiar resourcefulness, a peculiar 'way with words'. Wesker is not a poet like Arden; not a witty juggler of words like Stoppard; not a writer of pregnant silences like Pinter. There is something altogether more transparent about Wesker's language. There is something indeed 'unfashionable' about it. Something? . . . Something which other writers are unwilling or unable to give? And what is that?

33

Bewilderment. (Good word that! The dictionary gives the ancient root as 'wilderness': to be put upon *by* wilderness.) Bewilderment in real life may be tongue-tied, confused, even mute. But to uphold the view that 'bewilderment' *in art* cannot be bewildered; and, moreover, to uphold this view because it is the only way open to preserve genuine bewilderment — *that* is what makes Wesker seem unfashionable.

What in heaven's name do I mean by such double-talk? Well, let me put it another way. Wesker is willing to concede much to bewilderment — bewilderment as a reaction to *being* in this world. But the one thing he is not willing to concede to bewilderment is its *expression* in art. Paradoxically, Wesker's way of expressing bewilderment, and thereby preserving it, is to supply it with clearer words than might be the case in real life. (Wesker, reading this, would say: 'You forget that I often write about Jews — and Jews are only too good at expressing their bewilderment.' Maybe so. But this appeal to a peculiarity of 'Jewishness' stresses my point: exceptional articulation which in most other cases would remain nearer the zero-level of inarticulation.) I don't say such a form of expression is unrealistic. From that point of view, no art is 'realistic'. But Wesker sees no reason why the *potential* of art has to be 'choked' by any further increase of obscurity or mystery.

Note: I am not trying to put other writers down. Nor am I trying to pass Wesker off as martyr or uncanonized saint of reason. There are other writers of bewilderment, of despair darker than anything Wesker ever conjures up. Despair is the negative of hope (as in a photograph before the positive is developed). The black emotions expressed in modern art, the horror, the genuine despair, are after all precious. Why? Because art can still express *astonishment* at the predicament we are all in. Better to possess such astonishment than any amount of soft soap or facile optimism or sentimentality. Better, because it authenticates the positive within the negative itself; and, yes, it still holds out for hope, in spite of all appearances. Unfortunately, despair can become a style; it can be lightly worn. It can become *professional.* There is no longer any bewilderment about any predicament. Despair turns traitor and becomes cynicism which professes surprise that anyone can still be surprised. (Cynicism is supposed to be immune to any attack by surprise — like any good anti-riot squad. And *that* is indeed its role: to police anxiety, in the sense of administering it *for* and *to* others.)

Wesker at no point succumbs to the necessity of evil. That's what I'm really trying to say. What do his characters grapple with? Ignorance, yes, and corruption, cruelty, defeat. Yet there is always possible recovery. The despair is never total. Earlier on I mentioned irony — the influential sort which is an expression of the elite anxiety to keep others impotent. We've had an overfill of that. Newspapers provide us shovelfuls of horror. The need is for art which helps give shape to experience, and not more cynicism to bury us alive under helplessness.

Keeping bewilderment clear; keeping expression open, at least potentially — that's what I'm trying to say is different about Wesker. People in his plays may grope painfully. They may be confused; but they always express themselves openly. The more accurate term than 'openly' would be *explicitly*. Explicit — as in fact someone once complained about Wesker's style of playwrighting: 'You say what you mean!' This criticism (by a theatre professional who should perhaps have known better) displays its own level of bewilderment. It seems Wesker's defect that he believes the passage between saying and meaning should remain clear.

Here Arnold Wesker adds a '3rd person' comment:

He doesn't say it always can or will, or that it's even always desirable. But in calling for 'an initial vocabulary for understanding the human condition,' he adds: 'I do not say guaranteeing an understanding of the human condition, nothing can guarantee that! But a basis, upon which there exists a possibility for understanding . . . Despite abuse and all that has been done to language and committed in its name . . .'

Wesker's essays and plays are full of such temperings: no guarantee, just maybe, a possibility, the chaos will always be there, the clearings become overgrown. His last paragraph in this essay is quite categorical. 'Panaceas, we've long agreed, there are none.'

> So his characters may commit the heinous crime of
> trying to say what they mean, but always in the full
> knowledge that they may be wrong, or have not
> actually succeeded in saying what they mean, or can
> have their meaning changed by a new thought, or by
> someone else's meaning, or by experience. Words may
> be *key* for him, but they're not sacrosanct or definitive.

To some extent, one can even sympathize with the critic's
disbelief. After all, it does appear harder and harder to stick to
the faith that people *can* say what they mean. But there it is —
Wesker holds a rationalist's view of language. What is the
alternative? To say that people cannot really 'put into words'
what truly ails them is irrational. What is denied isn't only the
capacity for language. Everything hinges on that 'truly' — what
'truly' ails them. And what does truly ail humanity implies
something that finally and utterly escapes them. It implies that
they cannot really *do* anything about it. Denial of words ends
— or really intends — to deny reflection and action. It is fatalism
with a fatal purpose . . . to reduce others to silence! As such,
it is anti-socialist as well as irrational by design.

Wesker's people *talk.* They are not resigned to silence. They
talk — not obsessively like O'Neill's derelict beings; not totally
'at a loss' like Beckett's minimal beings. Wesker's people *see*
meaning, even if they cannot always command satisfactory
expression of it. Words exist to steer by. Words actually lead
somewhere. No matter the spectre of near defeat, the let-downs,
ironies and bitterness of struggle, words conquer. Think of *The
Old Ones.* The sheer, physical weight of years, infirmity,
biological fate, threaten to overwhelm Wesker's old people with
despair. Yet language is an optimistic force even then. Or think
of *Love Letters on Blue Paper,* Wesker's recent BBC television
adaptation. There it is an old woman's discovery of words
which triumphs astonishingly over biological destiny itself —
over *death* itself, the most inexpressible of all. Finding one's
own voice is absolutely vital to the future of Hope. Contact
with the wonder of words, the primal astonishment of words,
turns people into visionaries. Once they have had that contact,

they can never entirely lose hope.

In *The Old Ones,* two brothers have fought a life-long language duel, each seeking quotations to hurl at the other. Optimist-versus-pessimist. Near the end of the play, Boomy, the younger of the two, quotes the terrible words of Ecclesiastes: 'And there is no new thing under the sun.' Beautiful, even if terrible words; but Manny, the elder brother, replies:

> I know it's beautiful but I can't bear people who quote it all the time. You have to earn the right to find the world a vain place. But he *enjoys* quoting it, he *loves* it, relishes it. Listen to him roll all that juicy gloom on his lips. 'All things toil in weariness' – aaah! All things, that is, except *him.* You don't catch him reciting wearily – no! There's an energetic ecstasy in *his* voice. He *loves* it. Pronouncements of doom. Revelations of futility. Declarations of life's purposelessness. Except for *him. He's* got a purpose. A lovely purpose. The easiest of all purposes – to inform that no purpose exists! Catastrophemonger!

I began by singling out the three outstanding preoccupations, labour, beauty and reason, which distinguish Wesker's work. These are the features of a socialist writer which I can better define by adding that Wesker is a critical socialist, not a vaguely 'humanist' one (against the threat of insult that term carries). In what way critical? To illustrate this, let me quote from another of Wesker's plays, *The Friends.* Manfred, one of the characters, suffers from what one might call 'knowledge anxiety', which increases with every new book he reads. Every new piece of information upsets and unsettles him. Manfred talks to another friend, Macey, about just such a new book. (The three dots interrupting Manfred's speech below represent lines spoken by other characters.)

> **Manfred.** There's a man here says that the coming of print gave man a one-dimensional view of the world and crippled all his other perceptions.
> (. . .)
> Ssh! He says 'the phonetic alphabet makes a break between eye and ear' and man has used this to change from 'the tribal to the civilized sphere' and 'since it's obvious that most civilized people are crude and numb in their perceptions' then it follows that the printing press has held back progress for five centuries and

we must start all over again to unify the senses.
(. . .)
Isn't that staggering? Now I find that one thought alone upsets
everything, every thing.
(. . .)
Macey. What's so staggering about it? What staggers me more is
that print has been around for the last five hundred years and
not only is two-thirds of the world still illiterate, but even those
who could read never did, and still don't, so where's his proof?
How can you be crippled by something you never engaged in?
Maybe it's the other way round? Maybe they got crippled
because they *didn't* read.
(. . .)
Manfred. But words act like dams, he says.
Macey. Nonsense! I've never heard such nonsense. Lovely
things like words? 'Languor' — listen to it. It sounds like what
it is — full of lingering and longing: 'languor!' 'Anguish',
'miasmatic', 'crackling', 'surreptitious', 'sonorous', 'asinine'.
Lovely words. Dams? Gates more like, to everywhere, to
every-possible-where. What else is there? Can you think of
something better?

The book which so worries Manfred actually exists. Wesker
hasn't made it up. It is Marshall McLuhan's *The Gutenberg
Galaxy.* Macey's reaction is a rational, common sense one — and
also an immediate gut reaction. Does he represent Wesker's own
views? With a rational artist (such as Wesker is), the appeal to
non-fictional response seems obvious. One easily imagines that
what Macey says is 'really' what Wesker says. However, it is less
a question of Wesker's *own* views than those 'typified' through
fiction, through drama, and based on the fictional limits of
fictional characters. Macey's response, then, is a symbol or
'representation' of critical consciousness. Or, rather, the
implications of critical consciousness are present, not the fully
worked-out critical reply to McLuhan's book. I don't mean an
essay which Wesker might or might not have written in place of
dialogue. (Potentially, artistic expression always contains the
outlines of non-fictional response — criticism, the twin of art.)
What matters is the audience being able critically to identify its
own views. For example: 'Here is a supposedly influential book,
The Gutenberg Galaxy, by a supposedly influential thinker,
Marshall McLuhan. He asks us to "start all over again" when we
know we haven't even begun yet. He blames "printing" as if it

was some kind of pure, abstract force on its own. As if *it* shaped social and political forces, rather than the other way round. Illiteracy is man-made. No form of technology — whether printing or television or radio — can provide a remedy for the injustice that two-thirds of the world population is illiterate. Why *are* so many illiterate? Not *what* did it — but *who* did it, and *why?* That's what we want to know! Don't give us this guff about "eyes" and "ears". Don't kid us about our "numb perceptions" when so many are being beaten into silence.'

Some may complain that this isn't refined enough to pass as critical consciousness. It only extends Macey's gut reaction. Good. So be it. Does being refined mean being anaesthetized? There is nothing very refined about Macey's dismissal of McLuhan — true. No flattery is necessary. McLuhan is exposed for what he is — a highbrow television salesman. But the worse that can be said about McLuhan's influence is that it increases the anxiety of those like Manfred who are uncertain of their knowledge. Such harm reinforces an elite power structure which has the 'mass-media' on its side. Despite that, McLuhan is harmful rather than 'evil'. Evil must be accurately measured, Wesker observes, 'or we might find ourselves drawing blood to drown a fly, when to spit would be enough.'

To be a critical socialist does mean, as Wesker himself says, 'defending' the conceptual integrity of words.

But does language *need* defending?

You would think — and yes, rightly — that there are evils enough in our world, catastrophes a-plenty, corruption, cynicism. Picking up a newspaper is almost an exercise in courage these days. But added to that, there is another evil — one which surmounts and at the same time attaches itself to all other reports of evil. One which is not local but diffuse. Something less easy to put one's finger on than the plain, brutal facts. Something which increases and secretly influences exasperation, anxiety, doubt. Something which works its mischief not only on a few individuals here and there, but on masses of people throughout the world.

What is this *other* evil? The abuse of language.

There is more to this question than we are usually led to believe. Corruption of language is not simply a question of good or bad grammar. Nor is it a question of maintaining standards against the inroads of dialect or slang. The claims of orthodoxy veil the real question — which is indeed about use. Or, I should say rather than use, *manipulation.* Wesker mentions Nazism and its deleterious effect on language. That's one example. But, since then, we've had others equally malicious. Think of the Vietnam war and *its* macabre vocabulary. What horrors do such jargon-terms as *body-count, free-fire zone, defoliation,* disguise? What unaccountable crime masks itself behind the cant term, *Vietnamization?*

The high-road to mass murder was long ago camouflaged by pseudo-technical verbiage . . . during the First World War, and later by Nazism, by Stalinism, and by the Cold War. The threat of nuclear holocaust is in fact greater today than ever before. But what part has the manipulation of language played in numbing our comprehension of this fact? Just think of these terms — *multiple warheads, strike-capacity, megaton, escalation* . . . those initials, ICBM, MIRV, and yes, the famous SALT talks. What a mirage of non-words! Language itself has been criminally exploited to lobotomize the ability to face facts. How nice to have, as Norman Mailer aptly puts it, 'the taste of aspirin in one's death.'

When Watergate flooded the American public with verbal garbage, the source wasn't only Nixon or his playmates. Years and years of lying it took to build up so much pus. Lying about Vietnam. Lying to the public about everything that matters. You may call it simply hypocrisy. But criticism has to be more specific than that. *Words* had to be manipulated, words invented, distorted, corrupted. Words not so much used, as poured like concrete: so that they became, literally, *unthinkable.*

We badly need a survival-kit of words!

Every now and again, someone — let's not say an artist or a poet, but just a *thinker* — comes along and says, 'Hold on. Think a moment. Would crimes against humanity be committed if the perpetrators really *said* what they *meant?* Did the Nazis *say* what they intended to *do?* Did Stalin? Do our politicians? Things were said which no way resembled the reality experienced. Therefore, is it not true that the evil action has to be prepared for first — always first — by perverting language? Once the mind is dulled, the act is poisoned. This is what we must see. Language is not passive, not neutral, not something we can ever take for granted. Either we use language justly or we will be badly used by it.'

Does language need defending?

'To speak a true word is to transform the world,' Freire says. We could do worse than start by considering a linguistic survival-kit.

Notes

1 Paulo Freire, *Education: The Practice of Freedom,* p.111. Writers and Readers Publishing Cooperative, 1976.

2 Arnold Wesker has recently joined the Cooperative as a writer-member.

3 Carol and Lars Berggren, *The Literacy Process: a Practice in Domestication or Liberation,* p.25. WRPC Pamphlet, 1975.

4 Paulo Freire, *Cultural Action for Freedom,* p.30. Penguin, 1974.

5 P. Freire, *Pedagogy of the Oppressed,* p.56. Penguin, 1973.

6 C. and L. Berggren, op.cit., p.15.

7 Freire, see *Pedagogy* op.cit., p.24.

8 Freire, op.cit., p.24.

9 Freire, see *Cultural Action* op.cit., pp.33–34.

10 Freire, see *Pedagogy* op.cit., p.57, on revolution as the 'prophetic hope' which corresponds to the historical nature of humanity.

11 Freire, op.cit., pp.60–61.

. . . some books available from the
Writers and Readers Publishing Cooperative

Little Girls
Elena Gianini Belotti

A lucid, lively study of
sex-role stereotyping: how
deep-rooted social prejudices
conspire to turn boys into
aggressive males, and girls
into submissive housewives
and mothers.
Greatly successful throughout
Europe, this book has
inspired a new series of
Feminist children's books.
h/b £3.00
p/b 85p

Sexism in Children's Books
Facts, Figures and Guidelines

Edited by Children's Rights Workshop

The articles collected in this
booklet analyze sexism in
children's books and present
powerful statistical evidence
of its frequency and range.
The McGraw-Hill Guidelines
show how to begin to
recognise and combat sexism
in literature and in the use of
language.
p/b 60p

After Deschooling What?
Ivan Illich

Re-issue of the original WRPC pamphlet with an important new introduction by Ian Lister.
p/b 35p

Imprisoned in the Global Classroom
Ivan Illich and Etienne Verne
In this follow-up to *Deschooling Society,* Illich reveals the hidden snares in the recent enthusiasm for education outside the school system. Illich criticises the 'institutionalisation' of the education process—whether in or outside the traditional school system.
p/b 45p

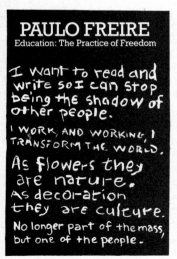

Education: The Practice of Freedom
Paulo Freire

This volume, now available for the first time in paperback, consists of two seminal essays by Freire, world-famous for his adult literacy method evolved in Brazil.
'Freire is one of the most important educators alive.' Ian Lister, *New Society.*
p/b £1.00

William Tyndale: The Teachers' Story
Terry Ellis, Jackie McWhirter, Dorothy McColgan, Brian Haddow

How the Tyndale teachers came into conflict with the educational authorities, the progress of the affair from initial crisis to inquiry, are all documented in detail and with vivid force.
p/b £1.00

Classrooms of Resistance
Compiled by Chris Searle

In this photo-illustrated book, Chris Searle brings together his pupils' poems, short stories, plays and drawings: the imaginative response of children aged 11 to 14 to such events as—the shutting down of Poplar Hospital, the Flixborough disaster, the murder of South African miners at Carletonville. A useful teaching vehicle.
h/b £2.25
p/b 85p.

LITERACY IN 30 HOURS
Paulo Freire's Process
in North East Brazil

Cynthia Brown

p/b 45p

THE LITERACY PROCESS
A Practice in Domestication
or Liberation

Carol and Lars Berggren

p/b 45p

The Journalists
a play by Arnold Wesker

Wesker's controversial play (which is presently the subject
of a lawsuit against the Royal Shakespeare Company) is a
dramatic account of the workings of a Sunday newspaper.
In special, magazine-size format £1.00

 **Writers
and Readers
Publishing
Cooperative**

For further information and our new 1976-77
catalogue write or phone:
**Writers and Readers Publishing Cooperative
14 Talacre Road, London NW5 3PE
Tel: 01-485-1949/2026**